CAMEO METRO

KEN CHAMPION

CAMEO METRO

KEN CHAMPION

First published
November 2013

ISBN 978-1-291-63374-0

Cover: East End Children 1954

PENNILESS PRESS PUBLICATIONS
Website : www.pennilesspress.co.uk/books

For
Steve, Tim, Toby
Adam, Emily & Isobel

Acknowledgements are due to the editors of the following where some of these poems or versions of them have appeared: *Rialto, Magma, Smiths Knoll, African American Review, Miracles and Clockwork* anthology: *The Best of Other Poetry, South, Bellevue Literary Review, Mistress Quickly's Bed, The Crazy Oik,* and others too numerous to list.

His accomplished style creates a poetry that is acute of observation, rich in memory, poignant, yet full of humour for the absurdity of everyday happenings. Over the many years he has wrote poetry he has become comfortable with his work, but his vocabulary isn't cosy, nor is it precious. There is a constant challenge in his poems… his acute use of the vernacular keeps the reader aware and attuned to his direct, un-flowery observations.

Les Robinson, Director, Editor, Tall Lighthouse (2013)

BUT BLACK & WHITE IS BETTER (Tall Lighthouse 2008)

This is an outstanding debut collection with some exciting poetry. Here is a writer who deserves to reach a broader readership.

Jim Bennett, Poetry Kit Book of the Month (2010)

These are gritty, urban, contemporary poems of a soulful and ironic nature, sometimes speaking of unrequited lust in a voice that is immediate and compelling. They are relevant to our changing society. Many reflect in a kaleidoscopic way the poet's travels. They are finely wrought lyrics.

Robert Cole, Editor, Chimera (2008)

Everyday objects and occasions explode into ideas and emotions in this muscular and very welcome first full collection.

Peter Bennett, Other Poetry Book Recommendation (2010)

CAMEO POLY (Tall Lighthouse 2004)

I've just read an excellent book of poetry by Ken Champion... All of our lives can be turned into the stuff of poetry, but Ken Champion has proved himself a master at neatly denying the expected, and serving up well-observed vignettes with no fear of us not appreciating them.

Peter Burnett, Sphinx Poetry Review (2006)

This is sassy, vibrant, streetwise poetry that cuts to the chase with verve and wit. Acutely observed, these poems are sensually engaging and likeable, like spending an evening with a good friend over a bottle of crisp wine.

Catherine Smith, The Frogmore Papers (2005)

Once more bridging the continents of Europe and Africa... Cameo Poly features some true gems.

James Melrose, The Ugly Tree (2005)

AFRICAN TIME (Tall Lighthouse 2002)

... the characters and incidents immediately focus the reader and tend to linger in the mind. They intrigue and often fascinate, especially the African girl whose relationship with the writer appears as a kind of narrative interspersed with poems of irony and loss. An excellent collection of poetry.

Jeanne Conn. Editor, Connections (2003)

CONTENTS

Rewind   99

Titles Index   115

City

Freedom Fighter

She walks easily
hijab swirling
in a breezy London park
her gaze straight ahead
on the angry back of a husband

An Islamic possession
she quietly knows
that her cover-up
is as useless as its irony
as her eyes catch mine

and I stop and imagine
dark nipples and smooth legs
as she moves away
female and hidden
in that oppressive black.
And her Nike trainers.

Pereidolia

the psychological phenomenon of seeing
meaningful connections in random objects

Staring at the platform wall, Victorian bricks, tiny indents
like the cave-pocked hillside where grandpa George hid
Maria from the *paseos,* thin mortar - Skinny Gwen's legs
hop-scotching between the cracks, smoothness of the
newel post orb, a ball dribbled round a streetlamp,
marbles clacking along the gutter

Fluted up-lights become Corinthian columns, me falling
as the ladder slipped, ticket window's *Art Nouveau* tiles
turn into a city whose boulevard trees are not high
enough to see from the *Sacre-Coeur,* the heels
of a passing woman, like yours, but not scuffed
by the heartbreaking limp

Outside, sky, dove of an evening cloud
silhouetting the hedge when dad died, red plastic
forks in the *Station Café,* the Devil in the detail.

Paseos: executions during the Spanish Civil War

Hawksmoor Church

It isn't precious, no Catholic gold and glitz,
just white columns, acanthus leaf, rams horns,
dulled oak - a sparrow would look down on grey

heads, black coats, wheelchairs, corner painting
and tomb, hear a violin dirge in a square nave
that's housed hatreds, saccharin cant, that's

never seen a floral *granddad* nor crossed
hammers in claret and blue roses; and this
before the spirit's weakening to the body,

the fidgets, coughs, desire for the wine and
smoked eels, toilets, *match of the day*...

Old Money

Finding the coins, the tupennces, two bobs,
it's their *clink,* their light ales, ten Woodbines,
dad's second-hand pintable, his walking across

the Thames from work seeing the flashing sky
not knowing if it was an incendiary'd street
his home no longer there, the beery, fake laugh,

one of the lads, honorary cockney, me in bed,
foetal, fists over ears, *that fuckin' boy,* the escape
across the heath, flinging myself into the grass

trying to push through the earth, his greyhounds,
mum's, *you think more of them than me,* his grunting
five minute Saturday night love; the pennies, their

brownness, their *britt omn rex fid def,* and his face
tinged by the swelling, fading light from the east,
fists clenching the change in his pockets.

Café E.10

There's a church opposite seen from under the awning
Alice the waitress sits outside with a cigarette
her smoke blowing across the open door
photo of the lunching riveters astride
a New York girder tilting on the wall
bright leaves on the graveyard trees

I hold up a scrawled phonetic of a Romany hello
she frowns, shakes her head, mouths *bunaziua*
the only movement now inside or out:
its owner, legs apart, looks at nothing
a customer stares at his cappuccino froth
the local butcher, grey hair thick at the back,
chin resting on a hand.

And you want to harvest it, bind it,
carry it home, place it on a sill in the sun
sit and look at it all, slowly, considerately;
Alice passes me as I rise from the table
la revedere she says
lahreveedaree I reply.

Equus

Hefting tins of lead paint from the yard across the
bridge, the Square, the job, *need a licence to shit
in the road, work like an 'orse,* says the guv'nor.

On the scaffold, chisel sable, inch tool for the
ceiling rose in red, fitch for the leaf green ovolus
low sun through windows lighting dust sheets,

softening the cornice, frieze; the light, the glow; I'm
Botticelli, Rafaello, want to lie on my back, stretch
an arm to guild the swags, tint the darts; I step back

into nothing, buttocks, head, hitting ladder rungs,
sprawl on the herringbone floor, paint spotting
around me, bright, like an animal's blood.

The Social Class Of Trees

It's their shapes, fan palms, monkey puzzles, the rich
greens, the Highgate Hill of them, fresh leaves hiding
fin de siècle gables, overhanging goggled motorists,
a plaid lapelled entrepreneur, waist coated Chief Clerk

smiling up through branches, the bright jade light then
downhill east, trees knuckled, dry, council-pollarded,
coalman bending sacks on his shoulder over a doorstep
chute, below, a boy standing on the settling coal, cellar

blurred by dust, running out to a horse pulling a carted
carousel, rides for jam jars, shrimps and winkles from
a barrow. The mother - apple of a street bookie's eye -
a daily herring and bowl of tea seamstress sewing

leg of mutton sleeves, lining merry widow hats,
her son playing in a sandpit, looking up; a veranda
glimpsed on the hill, mullioned windows reflecting
the sun, high chimneys, a sunlit, jacketed shoulder
on a camomile lawn, and the splendour'd trees.

White Marble Nudes

Stained rocks rise from a pool by the
Thames, atop, two rearing horses,
the chariot between their spread wings
driven by a female, whipless, hair
held high between her fingers,

a maid stretches an arm in worship,
a kneeling nymph helps up a friend,
their arms clasped, another sits in a shell
where, between finger and thumb, a nut
for a horse or pearl for the charioteer.

Arms wide, a girl bends backwards
as if suddenly aware of the animals
above, a lass below leans over the
water, surprised by her reflection, and
as the tide rises, weeds wash up to an
ankle, behind a knee, the palm of a hand.

On the other bank those that look across
may see only a tip of stone above trees,
a curl, a tress, not thinking there could
be figures here larger than life,
elegant, playful, drowning.

Ownback

Do you still love me,
I'd asked, grinning tentatively.
What's love? she'd answered
as she unlatched the door.

It *could* be, she'd said, a reference to the
God cupid with winged bow and arrow or
in evolutionary terms a mammalian drive
or perhaps a disambiguation...
Her sneering irony had trailed away
by the time she'd reached the gate.

Now, as I slope through London streets,
a foreign tourist asks me, 'What is time?'
It *could* be, I say, money or standing
still or flying by or a pre-arranged
moment for something to happen or
perhaps the space-time continuum
within quantum physics...

Laburnum Avenue

The sunray gate, garden steps, rockery either
side, the front door's leaded glass yacht, the
zigzag wallpaper, swallowing dry cake from

a Clarice Cliff plate, feet hardly touching the jade
and black carpet, a *don't ask don't get* nudge from
mum, tense with sister Joyce, easier with Con's

smokers cough and betting shop opposite, and
back to our tin bath, leather strapped ashtrays,
parlour's antimacassar homage to respectability;

walking the city now, still seeing curved bays,
herringbone bricks, Court foyers and chrome,
chevrons and pantiles and, somehow, smiling

auntie Joyce, her bright lipstick, tilted hat,
green fox fur, the glance down at me, that
look in her eyes, the recognition...

Café Gallery, E8

Like a 20s Russian émigré on *Rue St Michel*
she sits outside, cloche hat framing dyed hair
gloved hand emerging from blue angora
dabbing a tear from a pencilled eye
wishing her lovers to carry mobiles
so she can text how late she'll be

Art fanciers pass her, one fedora'd waving
his stick, retrospective critic; she moves
slowly, standing almost upright,
small, thin, switches on her phone,
wishes it was a samovar.

Game

Must fly, I lie, to Toby and Mo's,
Told them I'd stay a few days
I'll ring when I'm back.
I never do. I never go. I say it to all of them
Datelinedotcom women.
They like the ad.

Tall, attractive professional male,
sensitive, caring, into art and poetry
likes cosy nights out, exciting nights in.
I then add, *if you* intuitively *feel we have*
things in common, give me a bell.
They love that.

I'm good on the phone, laid back on the couch,
Seductive tones, old patter for new intros.
Ugandans are pleased when I recognise Acholi
or goldbangled Nigerians their fat, deep chuckles.
And a Mauritian is delighted when I use a little French
whilst a Watford widow feels a *frisson* of fire
when I tell her I look like George Clooney at forty.

But they're never quite right; too small, old, fat, cold,
fraught, short, short of cash, short of brain
(like the one who told me she was beautiful *inside*)
or too persistent, insistent, a mere rumour of humour.
'though I've just finished chatting to a slim five seven
ex-model therapist with a voice so soft
a plastic phone was too brutal for it.

I suggested Tate Modern, we could eat there, too.
Love to, she breathed, but I've promised a friend
I'd stay the weekend.
But I'll give you a ring.
When I get back.

B Feature

Away from the books and blinds
of Hampstead roads
Pre-Raphaelite hair swirling
as she jogs on the Heath
she stumbles and falls

at first in slow motion
then in realtime
sliding on her breasts through a puddle
fist delicately resting on a can.

I run forward slipping in the grass
as she raises herself on all fours
like a reluctant bitch
answering an owner's impatience
her face turned towards me.

I kneel and absurdly wipe the mud
from the tip of her nose
then grinning she suddenly stands
and runs on through the trees
while an old man with a backpack
frowns down at me,
as if knowing my life
is full of pointless cameos.

Postcard

In Paris streets
grills gush water along culverts
washing cobbles all day,
yet still surprises me
trickling around a corner.

And on boulevards
chestnut and plain trees
fill the city, almost touching
eaves and scrolled verandas,
but are not quite close
nor tall enough.

Here, away from
your screeching eyes,
I look across from the hill
to get an overview
of both the city and you,
unaware that I cannot
see the trees from
the Sacre-Coeur.

End of Terrace, 1669

In the strangeness of the first street of row houses, a resident
seeing opposite walls as his, chances upon blueprints (developer's
tears of triumph still moist) of forty one parallel lines demarcating
forty homes and, realizing the deceit of psychological ownership,
what if he knocks at his neighbour's to tell him that one of his walls
isn't his, is arbitrarily owned, then, vexed, returns to punch
a dividing one, plaster crumbling, distemper flaking, leaving the
neighbour, suddenly insecure, to flail fists against friezes, wainscots,
their movements almost synchronised as if they could see each
other, then both running along the road carrying the word that
the ownership of walls is in doubt.

Then all are attacking walls, hammers, picks, pokers, boots, lathes
torn away, bricks dislodged, the first hole knocked into a parlour,
bloodied hand showing through, ceilings sagging, glass exploding,
roofs splitting, falling, leaving them in a dust-fogged streetscape,
in a rubbled wasteland, undivided…

Caffe Ponti

It's hot, boat seats glisten like
lanterns, silver fire reflections
ripple under the bridge, *Si, pasta,*

grins Maria, I sit; on my way
to Dr. Jules, he'll insist again
that *all* creatures fear attack

and lean forward, head pecking,
mimicking fearful eyes, arms
like wings ready for flight,

Hey, she says, *cibo, mangialo!*
you eat like a bird.

It's so hot.

Southern Comfort

It's outside the station, floodlit, skim of water on ice,
a thin-bladed, arms flailing, arse falling, leg-splayed
shrieking place; rap beats around it, he can't see through

the noise, pushes into the crowd, it's solid, cold, hears
'it 'im, Wayne, gets to the crossing, half-way and suddenly
he's on all fours, looks up, people frowning, disapproving,

walk on around him, a pit bull turns its face into his, lead
held by a Burberry clad teen, *kicked my soddin' dog,*
her mate sneers down, the scramble up, the scrabbling,

clears his head, heart thumping, jeans torn at the knee,
near the cinema now, Silver Screen, two quid for tea and
biscuits and *Jezebel,* Alabama dudes raising hats, bowing,

verandas, embroidery, heat, *sho' is Miss Julie, yes'm*
Miss Julie, yes'm… sits gently down, sinks into his seat.

Constructs

I look at the skyscraper cluster across the
Flats, the cliffs of glass, thinking I can
see my children's reflection, wanting

to know them again, trying not to lay
fragments of my fake self onto them,
accept that they think I am older than

they, that a host of encounters have let
them rise like rockets; I lay on the grass,
look to the pyramid tops, imagine floors

full of their pictures - the eldest holding
a bowed branch, his brother trying to fit
a cleft twig to the string, in another the

youngest, eyes lilting on a butterfly, and
they're floating from windows, curling,
coming nearer, visiting.

Pastry

In Jones's, 'Remember Cookes's? got dun
fer 'orse meat.' 'Nah, best beef 'ere, mate,
licquor and mash, freeze it, goes to Spain.'

Dos caffenado con leche John. Chantelle,
not that spray again, get a real tan 'ere,
don't be a prat all yer life, 'ave a day off

The Sagrada, Nou Camp, Caravaggio,
Raul, flamenco, scrolls and God

Off fer me pies, Chant, see if Mario's
got some eels

Chimneys

Their London stocks, lipped pots against
a yellow-grey sky, slate roofs, childhood;
as if looking across from the slag heap

to terraced streets, lamplights, Alma Arms -
dad coming out to bribe you with a penny
arrowroot, *if you was the only gel in the world*

aunts with flappers hair, *who's a pretty boy?*
mum's *don't look, son,* as Joan from next door
breastfeeds her baby, the crush on Wendy

from over the road, fear at seeing her
parents kiss because yours don't, the
Gothic psychiatry, the lost marriages;

and it's spinning around like a reeling
carousel, my slag heap turning
into a hill of beans.

African

Buse Mncube

In a train on a first date
to see *Umoja* she wears
a velvet hat and reads a newspaper
and I ask if it's an African thing.
We don't show love or hold hands
she says and with her soft Zulu 's'
asks if my sons are well.

She revels in disinterest; not asking
who I saw a film with but where,
not who I was with in Paris
but a polite raising of an eyebrow
and on her fifth visit in a year
the expressionless gaze in bed
with legs rigid as if wired together.

On my towpath walk she glides by in a boat
a young African's arm around her
and I resist running to keep up with
her dark eyes looking void into mine
short hair unmoved by the breeze
lips soundlessly shaping the words
'How are the boys?'

Atheist at River Of Life Pentecostal

Driving with Tapo, twelve, and he knows the short cuts,
industrial streets, factories, dishevelled gym, and there are
the signs, neon strips, day-glo - churches competing for
God, Thandi whispers - and on the ground floor there's

Living Gospel Of Christ, two hundred arms rising, go to the
next floor, tell Tapo I got lost, Jesus will find you, he says,
smaller space, preacher in cream-coloured dress, *okome aka
bababa*, a seven year old in a pin-stripe pacing in the audience,

eyes ordering us to pray, year-old Emmanuel jumping up and
down on his chair to the music, singer soft-shoe shuffling across
the stage, Tapo playing drums, the girl in the corner, high cheek-
bones, an Acholi Beyonce, spread fingers turning into rhythmic

fists, the pastor suddenly here, large man, messianic, bass
voice rising, You must fear the Lord he glowers at me, then
softer, sensing a convert, Christ is waiting, let him in; just a
quiet keyboard now, Thandi kneeling, *Hallelujah, Hallelujah*,

and as Tapo guides us back I smile smugly, knowing that
after the tea and biscuits I beat the pastor at ping-pong.

African Analysis

You're *embracing* your pain, he hisses,
Non-o has gone (her lover's name has
clicks added to consonants),
without him you don't know *what* you are.
He follows her upstairs, his drink-driven
psychologism clenched in a fist.

> my uncle said I was spoilt because
> I didn't sweep the yard and cook tomatoes
> in the big pot like the other children and
> when I go back they ask for money
> and I give them and my aunties everything
> even my knickers - I came back on the plane
> wearing none - and can you lend me your
> T-shirt, you know I cannot sleep naked.

She lies down, her back to him, braided hair
in a loose knot on her shoulder
before flowing down almost to her hip.

> I am a wounded soldier
> making love on the battlefield
> she whispers.

Architecture

Regency, surely, Italianate tower, curved bays,
scrolled balconies, the painted render, panelled
doors, black and white diamond paths, there
a cornerstone year, Victorian after all.

I wish to become those roofs, look down to the
street, porticoes, clicking gates, behind to gardens,
a birch higher than me, unexpectedly the park,
watercolour lake, the bench by our gazebo.

I would look into my own loft at the joists, tank,
photos in a painted case of your African eyes,
braided hair, full lips, the sound of your harsh
vowels; I don't want to breath any more
your exotic air, I wish to be these slates,
firm, aligned, indifferent.

Going Native

For a while as you wake
you are the scent of Africa
a dark mystique in the minds
of missionary novelists,
glowing eyes
mouth a full-lipped enigma
Zulu buttocks like breasts
long black beauty fingers.

Then you change
you shrink, bowed
your look forlorn
braided extensions
no longer pluming
but sadly hanging
and as you leave
become the careworn
care worker you are.

But when you return
I want you to be tall and proud
lifting lashes that sweep me away
not meekly smiling
making me signal that I want you
by a grunt and a kick on your calf.

Social Scientist

Try telling three dozen African females
that God didn't create us, we created God
he tells the staff room, and of course,
they've never heard of Marx, he sneers,
as he strides to his class.

Ideas, he shouts; family, state, religion,
socially constructed. We're talking positivism,
determinism, sense-data.
He struts, half crouches and spins back
to the board, his marker slashing across it,
using it as a *tabula rasa* analogy of man.

He rolls his eyes when a student slides in,
his bellowing heard two departments away
as he grabs the register to demand his name.
Adam, the youth stutters.
But he needs an Acheampong, Kojali,
Abegonde or Okoti,
not a Christianised forename
of ubiquitous Catholicism.

The latecomer walks to the back of the room,
sits next to a girl with an apple on her desk.
The others look down.
Hiding their grins.

Girl, African

She walks in with a parcel
of stuffed fish-heads and yams
and begins washing up while they warm
and casually sucks one of the eyes
while I open the wine and watch her
take off the trainers that make her limp.

Her smile pretends to like my music
and there's the usual bedroom struggle
to remove her clothes
until she clamps my wrist
and I notice the rag around her waist
which, she has said, she wears for fasting
and she still hasn't spoken a word.

I remind her that last month
it was the blood that had stopped her
because it was against her beliefs
and now it's *more* religion, and will it,
I ask, be a headache next time.

She dresses swiftly,
her Nefertiti head upright and still,
and with a flat-vowelled finality
suggests I write a poem about it,
and soundlessly leaves the house.

Retro

40's Noir

It's the lighting; a beach hut's sculpted shadows,
a white face pushing from a darkened porch,
Mitchum in Acapulco heat, slatted light

across his jacket, Greer walking in against the sun,
a Mexican Dietrich strolling a highway, headlights
stroking her back before she becomes night,

the palms, fedoras, wise guys, bars;
the evening park, a tram's *Nighthawks* figure,
kids playing floodlit footie round a lamppost,

the hall glow through the fanlight, lincrusta,
dad's torch searching the cellar for the nail jar,
Aunt Flo upstairs hoping I'll pencil a seam

down the back of her painted legs while
Uncle Harry's away, her face under mine,
garish, by the cheap bedside lamp.

Conservation Area

The pavement trees weren't there then, nor the
leaded glass in the Brown's cricket-balled fanlight
and the rugby pitch in place of the sandpit, swings,

the see-saw escape from god-fearing Gothic that pressed
us all flat, booted, open collars over sports jackets, and
high skirted Jeannie dancing past Fat Freddy's to the

sweet shop, footballer-owned *Alma Arms, Dellmura's*
ice cream, public baths, Sykesy and me smashing
a window, ripped hand still scarred, nor the slatted

blinds, matt front doors, the awninged Latvian deli
comfortable as a Paris street corner, but the City
Corporation sign at the park entrance proudly black

in the sun remains, with the genitals I chiselled on its
edge when I was ten.

Period Piece

They're looking at a house, arguing whether
it's Victorian or Edwardian - one points out the
former's yellow stocks, slate roof, cannon head
chimneys, the other, the latter's multi-paned sashes,
veranda, fish scale hanging tiles

as if there is a moment when a house must change
from one style to another, that the foreman, learning
of a Queen's death, would carry on helping a mason
lift a gargoyle, tell labourers to continue mixing
cement or shout for them to cease

a carpenter to lay down his saw, bricklayers their
trowels, carry them home, bossing mallets, hammers,
ask them to wait till a decision be made, perhaps
to start again, the blueprints, young architect,
cravatted, elegant, foreman calling at cottages
rounding up his men

They walk on, laughing at their pedantry,
leaving a charge hand long gone,
a house in confusion.

Banjo

Skinny and twelve in Peg Leg's east end garden
where he swings his good leg a second after the
wooden one almost upright above parallel bars,
biceps taking the load

C major he shouts, *Move*. Then the end of his peg
kicks back and me angling my head to miss it.
His pendulum body slows, drops to his only foot,

points me inside to make some music while his
roaring *get on with it* attacks the room with its
gas mantles, and ashtrays strapped on armchairs

and I *every-good-boy* it, tune up with cloth ears, strum
awkwardly, thin voice humming *Goodnight Ladies*.
Back in its case I'm ready to walk home close to walls,

avoid other kids - learning music, like big words, sparks
the screech of hatespeak - crush my school cap into a pocket,
hear the creak of bars and now the scream of shells, wonder
if, rifle in hand, he huddled against trench sides.

Dad's Dog

In the cafe with the others, pressing, squinteyed.
Gotta chance 'as it? gonna win? Charlie, *Gets
out the traps quick, does it?* Wag sails in, fists
pumping, *'it that lid six, go on my son.*

Can hear Johnny, *Nah, she wouldn't let 'im
near 'er, pissed I fink.* Sits down next to me.
Finish in front, will it? Site agent in the corner
Man o' the moment, eh? they buyin' yer tea?

Sykesey's brother, *'ope it runs faster than
you cut in sashes.* Guffaws, heads back,
snared teeth, spittle. *Be of some fuckin' use
then, tell us.* Hear Billy at the counter, *Airship
on a cloud, luv.* Turns his head, *Romford, an' it?*

Come on, chrissake, 'orse's mouf an' that.
It's a dog, I say. *It can speak then. Can't
paint windows though.* Foreman rising. *Let's
do some, it's a big ceilin', long run till tea.*

They squeeze past him. Two strides back, face
into mine. *Better not cross that line in front if we
ain't on it.* Leave my babies on a raft to get cold.

Hit that lid: *If a greyhound leaves the traps very quickly
theoretically its head will hit the inside of the rising gate.*
Airship on a cloud: *'sausage and mash'.*
Babies on a raft *'beans on toast'.*

Billy The Kid

Billy was the smartest kid around
at playing dead.

Blow a hole in his chest with a .45
and he'd hurtle six feet backwards
and lie perfectly still till his
mother called him in for tea.

Pierce his tank turret with a shell
and bits of him broke off
as it ricochetted around
until there was hardly any of him left.

Send him over the top and
he'd kill twenty Germans
before falling back in the mud
dying slowly and heroically.

Give him a mission impossible and
he'd return dragging the entire armada
before life oozed from him
lying face down on the beach.

And he could choke to death brilliantly
if you strangled him.

Father, Son, Holy Ghost

I'd sit there staring at the tin bath on the fence, mum
creeping between table and kitchen, *Don't do that Alf*
she'd say as he picks his teeth with a match, and Tony's
not home and if I walked across the park thinking of his

drawn-curtained house the trees would spin in panic,
kids sand pit stretch like a desert, so I leave under the
cracked fanlight to catch a train up west, gaze at Georgian
windows, the magic of Art Deco curves, the bend of

a Regency terrace, cluttered chimneys regressing to perspective,
a spire, churning memories of sitting in pews next to dad's
sharp elbow, *Fidget arse, keep bleedin' still,* the fake reverence,
lips out of synch with hymns, pious lectern, vaulted silence,

and years later in the same church atheist Tony and me with the
Africans, *We live in the age of the spirit,* quotes the pastor, *ahaba
ashab, obeke* - speaking in tongues, says Beauty - and the drums,
chorus, keyboard, devotional karaoke from the screen, Tina Turner

sound-alike vibrating the walls with passion, flicking a high-heeled
foot, behind her a golden *Holy God Almighty* across a mural of
flowing hills, phalanx of pilgrims crowding towards the foreground
river - if God existed he'd live in her legs, whispers Tony - Beauty

pushing past us, tumbling out her testimony into a snatched mike;
and perhaps the kitchen still exists, but not the bath or the cracked
fanlight, though the path across the park is still there.

Street Games

Flinging the ball at the pennies - tanners if you're flush -
on the paving slab against the end house wall, and mum
shouting down the street for your tea, and you run past

the parlour to the kitchen, stir the washing in the boiler
with the bleached broom handle while she salts greens,
squeal of fork inside a saucepan, hand wiping a brow;

and you want to run to the park, past the playground.
round the bandstand, on to the Flats, jump the stream
between houses, lean on a fluted lamppost and sate

yourself on mind flicks of skinny Iris at number two
or the misty silken space inside the thighs of principal
boys your dad takes you to see at Lyceum pantos,

but knowing you're only going out to the coins again
that no-one ever seems to hit.

Lock

A bespectacled girl, her laugh lighting the cafe
like the sun, which hits the bridge, crossing
train, reflected trees, and you suddenly notice

the music, alien at first, then you're back at the
Palais - ballroom taught you by a teacher at tech -
leaning on a wall, draped jacket, Tony Curtis hair,

yellow teeth, fear; glitterball glints on lacquered
waves, flared skirts, *'ere, she might let yer give
'er a French kiss;* the girl in the glasses, eyes

straight at you; walk quickly away, *Jenny Wren*
tying up, the market, goths gear, rockers,
punks, the past.

Century

The crudely copied map, mistakes, *22 Poortway*,
the A13, estuary, bungalows, pylons, blood strangers
meeting mostly at funerals. There'll be Ernie and his navy
reunions, Keith telling us again he and Sharon have split,

Rose at the table's head, twinkly eyes and double entendres,
a reminder of her son and *Monopoly*, with me, tooth-braced,
losing, upending the board, hotels scattering across the rug
dad made and sending us shopping, comedy of errands, sword

fights up and down the street, gripping laths from shattered
homes, and pretty Polly the fish shop girl, sliver of glass,
scar highlighting her face, and Teapot Lil and stick-legged
girls; *where's da music, mun?* demands a great grandson,

'ere's to yer next 'undred aunt, someone will shout, and
as we leave, Len the clever one, will muse on what use
to evolution is the knowledge that we're going to die.

Napier Road

Don't know how it began; couple of kids in an east end school,
the bell ringing at the end of a lesson marking another round,
me drawing Spitfires, zigzag propeller circles, rushing out of Art

as he runs from the Science lab, punch his head, he pulls my hair,
hands smelling of bad eggs; run to our next class, he to Geography,
atlas upside down on meagre knees, thinks Paris the capital of

Rome, me to Woodwork, planing smooth a model racer, Mister May
smiling; miss him at break, probably writing fifty lines, *I must pay
attentshin*, see him after Maths - top again - as he runs towards me,

eyes wide, kicks out, then scurries off to R.I. me to P.E. where
I vault the horse, score two goals in a five-a-side and between
History and English pull him round the parquet floor because he

rakes my face with a pen he hardly knows how to hold, then the last
bell, and it ceases. Saw him recently, still lives in his council flat,
didn't answer when I reminded him, laughing, asked how it started.

Houses: anthropomorphic

Sun on pantiles, boughed leaves against a window
like a mother's hair touching an infant's face,
cupola, an offered breast, eaves, the brim of
a merry widow hat, full-bosom'd caryatide
the long skirt's folds for a child to hide its face,
jasmine hedge cushioning his boundaries.

Raised eyebrow of a high gable, railings, tall,
upright, *'old yer back up,* chequer pattern flint
and stone, tough, hard, *'it a six, son, you can do it,*
catch it, catch it, the steep pitched roof, thick
brows frowning down; a frightened boy,
his father's house inside him.

Bombsite

Found a wooden leg he kept throwing
in the air, brassiere full of rubble he swung
around his head, filled a bag with shrapnel
carried round for days.

"Alfie Herd did a turd behind the kitchen door
cat came up, licked it up, asked for 'apporth more"

Tall-funnelled ships docked at terraced ends,
streets like giant gangways,
the blast absorbed, still floating,
rocking slowly.

Smashed houses in fake perspective like
a monochrome stage set, neat garden,
pipe smoker leaning on a roller-coaster
fence nodding in sympathetic circularity
with a cardigan'd neighbour

Patterned paper walls, dado rails, fireplaces
standing atop each other - an art installation
in a wasteland,
little Alfie swinging his bra,
ready for Goliath.

Aunt Rose's Funeral

The copy of *Saga* on a sill in the chapel,
plate glass views of pylons, your greying
cousins, the Benfleet bungalow, the pampas

grass she would pick to spray with lacquer
for the vase, the disappointments, George
not understanding ethnomethodological

phenomenology, Ernie suddenly seeming
likeable, the surprises, Bill the shop steward's
reluctant Marxism, a granddaughter's mini

skirt and high heels, the clichés, *nice spread
Vera, she 'ad a good innin's, lovely service,*
and centre circle, Stan nodding, joking, and

you can't join in, and the screaming
imperative to intellectualize, and still
hearing her calling you *Kenny*.

Configurations

In front of him a Victorian tower rises from
the mist, balconies, quoins, Palladian roof,
stares at its arching curves, symmetrical

dusk-like loveliness, yearns to embrace it,
to hold on to bowed windows, glass starting
to sparkle as the sun twitches on glazing bars,

rests on soft bricks, high wisteria, pull it all
inside of him and not to wonder if the void
it would fill is shaped like the fist-smashed

biscuit tin at home or the ziggurat
of his father's knuckles.

Retro

Headscarf knot high on her forehead, henna'd hair,
shoulder pads, like a war poster; she becomes
Aunt Lil - smiling down, hand cupping my chin -
holding Sid's arm, evening drink in the Plough,
slabbed eels twitching outside, pillbox hat for
The Harold on Sunday, turban in the tractor
factory making shells, painted line down
the calf for the Rex.

See her again, red tights, trilby, Camden-booted;
I'm Uncle Albert, double-breasted, roll ups,
knees ups, nudge and a wink to Charlie,
pencil 'tash, flash of a gold tooth smile;
she walks away, looks back, frowns,
leaving a raggedy-arsed boy.

The Last Stroke

The ward was once a billet for men at the aerodrome
its Art Deco tower guiding aircraft into a black and white
film, and where it was filled with the smell of oil and fags
it's now urine struggled through in slow motion by nurses,

doctors, everything living. The sister says *sorry*, for no more
is he the man who never touched me in anger - never touched -
had carried me on mean shoulders calling me *son*, but never
my name, had played keeper for his regiment, hid behind trees

at the back of the school shouting, *dive at their feet!* as legs
like giant slugs marched towards my goal; in the days when
a Big Mac was a large raincoat the ball weighed more than me
and covered in grass and guilt I'd watch the big boys cackling

back up the pitch as I shamefully pushed a foot back into a boot.
Now he's strangely spread under a sheet, like a goalie, the ball
past him; in bits, like pieces of Spitfire scattered across a runway

Americana

Quincy - Chicago

Your son takes a picture of you in front of the Amtrak
one foot on a rail holding Billy in the crux of an arm,
and you say your goodbyes, his mother distant, bitter;

and there's other snaps in your head, the Catfish Place
sign against a criss-cross contrail sunset, matt black
40's Chevrolet in the foreground, Whitney for Sheriff,

No trespassing, violators will be shot, survivors shot again,
the good 'ol boys in the Mennonite café, *I dunno why but
he flew that thing straight into a barn,* tarred roads, yellow

smudges where the paint trucks veer off the lines, outside
the window, clapboard houses, wrap-around porches, acres
of dry wheat, highway diners with signed pictures of Dolly,

and you wonder if you'll see your grandchild again;
console yourself, knowing you'll tell everyone
you've been across the Flatlands.

Auction, Memphis

Two dollar bill two dollar bill da-labil da-labil da-labil

you wanna bid that fifty cent crate Larry? we got
some pillers and sheets here Bentwood rocker
blue crock bowl and Bob stop strokin' that dress
she's gone now and ah put it there anyways
and yeh I shoulda gotten more fer yer house and
tractor too and Josh that woman o' yours
sure got a sparkle in her eyes these days, well she
has when she looks at me, boy, and Troy, livin' on
yer own now uh? well I got at least two, might
let yer share one, ha ha, and best keep yer womenfolk
at home next week those of yer still got 'em, it's mah
diamond-studded belt they lerv, and don't forget
we're over at Ray Bang's gun store then, and ah might
just have a mind to let yer bid for pieces o' yer lives back

Two dollar bill two dollar bill da-labil da-labil da-labil...

Dad's Grub

We walk Brooklyn Bridge, touring, laughing,
try a Bronx accent for their old East End ritual
waddya wan' Alf, two cheese, one o' jam, uh?
doin' a double shift tonite Edie, gimme a slice
o' bread and drip and a tomayta.

We're heading Downtown, but I see us all at
Clacton, knotted hanky on his head, paddling,
squinting at the sand, roll-up dangling from
his lip, mum square-jawed in a deckchair.

In front now, bruv's mimic of *that soddin' boy*
stops the laughter, it's still inside us: the brass
stair rods, silent meals, bent knife trapping the
gravy, *workin' it up,an' I,* the tassled table cloth,
echo of a key in the cheaply grained door, the
grim mat-stamping, shaking of a wet raglan.

He lets me catch up, turns his head, smiles,
silently mouths *bleedin' yanks,* we stride on,
the *Eastside Deli* straight ahead...

Deco Fair Junkie

There's a shallow cliff, storm-blurred palms,
at the edge of the print an *American Bar* neon,
a Bugatti silhouetted in front, and you wonder
if a man with a belted mac is standing inside

the door, fedora dripping, a bottle-blonde and
slicked hair charmer at the bar, dismay as she turns
her head, *No, Johnny* - the explosion sudden, alien,
wise guy tilts to the floor, she screams, hands

cupping her cheeks, the man walks out,
pulls up his collar, car splashes away
along Mulholland towards the valley,
trees sway wildly, fascia sign spluttering.

On the centre stand a stepped lamp seeming
higher than the others, its translucent blue like
a tower above a gold-studded Chicago night,
theatres, ballrooms - a club, Lempicka mural

lit from the side, sharp suits tense at a table,
one nods, another leaves, sidewalk shadows lead
him up back-stairs, an open door, a body across
a bed, hanging auburn hair from a bloodied head

rests on a Valmier rug, a Diomode light triple-
reflected on a dressing table, outside, a chaotic
city, its rackets, two-timers, white-walled tires,
figured walnut, Lalique glass, fedoras.

Men's Store, Leanda, Missouri

It sells cowboy-fit jeans, tooled belts, stetsons, outside
below the Court House clock forever at four, Chevrolets,
Dodge pick-ups, and you're back in the fifties with Tony

watching *Giant, The Big Country,* talking about *The Man
From Laramie* for hours, and staring at a tart and her client
on the debris behind the *Windmill* where a man with pyjamas

under his trousers jumps over seats to get to the front, and
back to the movies, the fastest draw, City Hall corruption,
Burt Lancaster's teeth, Cyd Charisse's legs, then you

have to grow up when Tony takes Mary Dowsett away,
in your dreams you're still running after them
silently shouting, *Shane, Shane, come back...*

Model Soldiers

Wearing camouflage suits
matching tank tops and desert boots
Sam Brown belts
leather holster accessories

mandatory shades and optional berets
razor-edged flat to the sides
of Clooney stubbled faces
with grey cropped hair

rogering the rear of Havanas
with matches before suckling,
here they come. Mom's apple pie
colonels catwalking across the world.

Girder Men Photo

It's as if they're in the bleachers waiting for
a game to start, the one on the end cadging
a light from his buddy, another peeking at
a workmate's lunch, the cloth caps, boots,
East River beyond, Manhattan below.

Tomorrow the man at the side of the cable
is playing pool with Ed and the boys downtown,
the hatless one's with his dark haired Sue
at Coney Island, elbows jutting in *contrapposte*
burlesque giggling into a Kodak, the man with
the vest and the take-my-wife jokes *she's so fat*
wherever she sits she's always next to me drinks
at a bar in Hoboken, the rest of them in a theater
on Times Square, fight at Madison, a diner.

Then it's back to the metal, chains, the rivets,
the heaving, pushing, the grappling with
memories they can't hold, which float away,
snatched by the high wind below the steel.

Memphis Window Cleaner

He's drinking chowder when he hears the
siren, runs up Main Street to the blazing café,.
firefighters looking up at suntrap windows

he leathered that morning. He'd seen reflections
of pantile roofs, ridge tiles, thinking he could
see foyers of chrome and black, walnut and jade,

glittering spire of the Empire State, hear
Stardust on a sax; now sees the glass crack,
frames buckle. Back home he picks up his

trumpet, plays *Honeysuckle Rose,*
stares at his Lempicka on the wall,
can see it burn, edges curl...

Englishman Abroad

Harlem, where anti-fit jeans crotch at the knees
high fives on sidewalks, insults mocking across
streets, coffee with the old guy making it last
all day coughing on about sickness and soccer
the squeeze of my arm when I leave for the subway

Upper East Side cappuccinos, ice-packed fruit shiny
and sweet, rainbow filled wraps, Alastair Cookeians
wearing Abercrombie & Fitch, undergrad kids in
baseball caps, Barbours, girls in orange high heels
talk of books they bought in Barnes and Noble
whether its writers' mural was Americacentric

In the cab, realise both delis have
plastic knives.

Calls

He's just skyped me from a wet car park in Poulsbo,
once rang from a ditch near Toulouse where
he'd rescued someone in an overturned car,
from a Space Agency yacht on a Swedish lake,
and the trailer park in Memphis where his wife had
screamed at him, upsetting young Billy, where
we'd shared a wrap-around porch and the sound
of cicadas, then the Sheriff's car, Pete stepping out
drawling apologies as he drew out his handcuffs 'cos
Jeannie's made a DV complaint, the low-crotched
orange overalls for the 24 hour hold, not seeing Billy,
and me having to fly back; I want him to ring again -
from his rebel rag office with CCTV on a lamppost
looking in the window, or Effie's place in Norway or
the beautiful Moo's Sussex garden, laughing, quietly,
that crib chuckle when I'd feed him his bottle.

Theatre

Funny Girl

In charge, young as I was, of refurbishing
Streisand's dressing room for her six-week
stint as Fanny Bryce and working hard
for time to sit, overalled, at the back
of the stalls to watch rehearsals and
her complaining that her lunch box
was too heavy to hold.

The shouts for a new one
from director and cast echo away
in diminishing regress as her Bronx
impatience clears the stage, then suddenly
the soaring perfection of *People*,
the silence, the unscripted applause
including ours, as she finishes
professional and deadpan.

And her next song crushed short
by a demand from the circle
for the conductor to get it right
and he, like a nervous butterfly
claiming he was following the score
and the theatre filled with the rasp of
'I *wrote* the fucking score!'
On the way home the 'Standard's headline
of 'Jule Styne Sacks British Conductor'
does not carry the crassness,
nor the beauty.

Afternoon Movie

You go in knowing it's already started;
there's a close-up of a girl staring across
a stretch of water, profile, tear on her cheek -
this time you don't look for the camera's
reflection - then the static shot, full face

looking sad as she drives along a road,
not even the upward, arcing angle of tree tops
to lessen the intensity, and you wonder what's
happened to her, a father dying, a crushed child,
and you know that soon the scene will end,

she'll get out, technicians take the camera
off the bonnet, unit director smile and brush
her cheek as the chief grip laughingly drives the
car away, she'll light a cigarette, yawn, tell
a stunt man jokingly to piss off; all the time

that first shot of her is flooding your mind,
and you want to be with her, just with her,
looking across the water.

Cotton Documentary Short: Visuals

titles, intro and music agreed, commentary under discussion
long-shot London Bridge, morning rush hour; slow zoom
to walkers clothes: shirts, jackets, trousers; dolly up to grey
sky, merge into blue; lock down on white-tinted landscape;
mid-shot of head-scarved women filling baskets, grinning
to camera through mist of candy floss cotton; pan right
to plantation owner's beaming face, arms paternally spread
shots of females showing bruises from overseers' sticks redundant

cut to rolling lorries, drivers' thumbs-up from cab windows
to roadside camera; close-up of auctioneer's hammer; shot
of clapping bidders; mid-shot of looms, shaking, sifting haze
becoming thread; cut to rollers pressing out cloth; long-shot
of goods trains silhouetted against a tropical sun
grip's pics of 24 hour-shift drivers asleep at wheel not needed

aerial long-shot (helicopter) of slowly turning container ship;
upward arc of dockside gantry swinging container onto
truck; fade to exterior of shining new factory - CGI - trucks
unloading; cut to interior, young women, hair in buns,
chatting at machines; close-shot of spread fingers
positioning pockets, hems, labels; fade to reverse zoom
of opening shot, but with sunny sky
closing credits as agreed
gaffer's snaps of needle-pierced fingers
and footage of smiling soldiers at gates pretending to shoot him unwanted

Nike interested in product placement

Pedestal

In a Barcelona street there are statues that aren't real
they're people standing still
till the chink of coin elicits an arrogant turn of head
from a marble veined Columbus
or a smirking salute from a copper cast G.I.

And there's a bronzed centurion who raises his spear
and a golden pair of potentates who bow
as pesetas rattle their boxes
whilst a man made from chalk with a guitar and a scowl
merely plucks a string as a grinning tourist drops a cent.

But it was the girl made from lead
with an errant wisp of hair, spinning her
grey rose and blowing slow kisses
who entranced me into daylong gazes
at her Eliza Dolittle face and small sweet waist.

I brought her home a month ago
but it's too cold to play statues so she dresses up
and stands in front of our mirror perfectly still all day
until I come home and place a penny in her little box
when she twirls her drab rose and pouts her lips.

And when in bed I touch her leaded hand
she shrugs and murmurs in that Catalan way
I'm tired, I've been on my feet all day.

Usherettes

Some serve in a churchlike Athens Odeon, an act of observance
and Greek dubbing, others in Sao Paulo's Una Banco pimping
ice cream while waiters tout margaritas, a Tangier picture
palace where the audience shouts *look behind you!* to the hero,
comfort refugees in a shell-pocked art house in Beirut, watch
contraband movies in an Art Deco theater amongst Havana
palms, fight off the manager of the Roxy in Taiwan.

They've heard the roar of light hit the screen, ping of a bra
strap from the back row, watched a lit match passed like
an Olympic flame across red velour seats, cigarette smoke
floating into bas-reliefs and chevrons; torch beams gliding
over carpets they are ciphers guiding us into the city,
its mansions, bedrooms and bars.

There's one now, next to my aisle seat, raised knee flicking
off a shoe, leaning back on the curtained wall, unlit torch
idly hanging, the world at 24 frames a second in her eyes.

Matinee

Down Drama Studio stairs
and there she is thin and toothy
giggling away the interval
screaming water over student pals
until I shout them to a stop.
Last week she thrilled as Moll Flanders
today third from left in the chorus.

Classroom free for an hour
I sit darkened in the stalls
as they pass by to the stage
where she is tall and proud
and ten years older
as she groins tightjeaned
with a Travolta wannabe.

A lookalike for you
the thump of jealousy
is not for her.
And she wouldn't know
what a Stagedoor Johnny was.

Genre: Gangster

i.

close shot, lipstick-glistened,
mascara'd, leans forward,
rucked stocking over toes
unrolling, whispering, shining

ii.

flat road across wheat fields,
mid-shot following a Buick,
fedora'd silhouette, hidden
briefly by a farmhouse,
beyond the dusty yellow
rises Chicago, its towers pushing
into the pale air, curved back
of the car moving towards it

iii.

street lamp, a girl passes, turns into
an alley, cars swishing, receding,
camera gliding through a doorway,
moves jerkily up stairs, two men
struggle in a room, one crashes through
a window, the sound loud, sharp

the body sprawled on cobbles,
faint saxophone as if played streets
away, cut back to the room, tall man,
side of his face lit in the dimness,
We did it, Tilly, he's gone

down again, she's glancing up
from the alley straight at the lens,
smiling, turns, stilettos fading,
saxophone swelling

iv.

a *Pathe* newsreel of a scene
corpse in monochrome
white shirt, black trousers
dark blood drying on the head,
a woman stares at a gun, loose in her hand,
curve of the handle, colour, texture,
frowns in three-quarter profile, blurs,
a rising shoe sharply focused as the door
closes behind, she sits, leans forward,
picks up a stocking

Marat/Sade

I'd told the Japanese man with the
beautiful daughter reading Physics
that my son was in this and had
warned me not to sit in the front row
because the Director was adventurous,
and as the lights brightened we could
see what the silhouettes really were.

All the lunatics wore white shifts, hugging
themselves, swaying, some staring wildly,
others repeatedly standing and sitting
while Marat lay centre-stage in his bath.

And there was Steven kneeling before us,
thick black hair, gurning mouth, bare legs,
neck in spasm as a spotlight circles him
crawling up the aisle, yearning eyes on the girl;
next to me her father stiffens as the madman
reaches for her thigh, then throwing back
his head suddenly stands and with elbows
imitating chicken wings limps Quasimodo-like
back to the other inmates.

As the play's first lines are spoken
the Japanese man whispers, Who your son then?
He's over there I say.
No, the one in white.

At The Hop

Above the Thai Café it's Salsa Basics
and I can't step and count at the same time
but the chunky lady in red taffeta and black
laughs us through, whip your head under her arm
as if checking out her arse and hold her hand
as if you're having a piss and kick your leg
and rub your calf as if you're cleaning your shoe.

Then the entrance of an honorary Cuban shaking like
a dog shagging in the street and I drag you away
to grab refuge in a waltz and when salsa man
smirks, wrinkling his sideburns, I tell him they're
playing the wrong music and you pull away and
sway with him and I go back to our table and take
your poems from your bag and finding no solace in

Latino and *Rumba Rap* push between you and whisper
an impromptu limerick in your ear: a Cuban dancer
named Bruno said if there's one thing I do know
it's that a woman is fine and a sheep divine, but a llama
is numero uno, and in disgust you grab your bag and
push out through the door with the draught swirling
around and *Dancing Queen* settling at my feet…

Room

The times I've been to him, uphill from the
station, walking on the thin pavement, around
the tower because it's early, and again he'll
tell me I'm not psychologically born, cannot
separate, stalling the terror of *why?*

I cross the garden to his door, pause at the open
window, the cream walls, red valmier rug; he's
bending forward like a chess player, talking
to a man, *the realest thing to you is your pain,*
your fantasising seduces you, an escape,
a long compressed gaze, *you have a choice*
Mister Cavari, hand flicking away irrelevance,
we can talk of sex, the Oedipal, or we can skirt
around what you need to do - a frown, *skirt*
perhaps an unintentional slip; *so, do we play*
about and talk of, Cleo, was it? or begin your
journey back, to the womb.

If this was a movie it would be a static shot
from two metres before a pan away through
the window; the tall, handsome man crouching
towards the thin, hollow-faced one; a zoom
back, the camera trying to snare the mind
behind the eyes; and he looks up at me…

Brief Encounters

The brown carriages, waiting room,
porters, pistons, steam, the refreshment
room tea urn, hat stand, trilbies, fox furs,

the woman, respectable, pain in her eyes,
brave mouth, walking along a platform
towards the camera and away from her

almost-lover; the screen in the darkness,
front seats, aisles, usherettes at the back,
torches still, recognising the stifling duty

of their own Saturday night giving - bearing
the weight, smelling the Woodbines and ale,
and watching her straight back, shoulder pads,

wanting her to turn and run back to him, leap
through the smoke, rise above the sooted
columns, shatter the roof, soar...

The Reading

Pages of anthology held at her breast,
a heel rises, groin subtly gyrates as the voice
tells of skin, breath, touch, of crippled sheep,
skinned hare, of a husband who kills for her,
of meat, the splitting of her, of a beast
dragged inside her

I see her daughter at home trying on a cloche
hat, pinning a deed mouse to mummy's fox fur
smelling still of hounds, sneaking a foot
inside a snakeskin shoe, swaying to and from
a mirror'd reflection, daddy's axe in hand.

She smiles down at the caffe owner's boy
as they share an interval macchiato; perhaps
she'll take him home for Pippa.

Mis en Scene

Walking past the Tate I see a red phone box
that wasn't there yesterday with a man gazing
out at a camera through empty glazing bars
and interrupt the director's *Actionez!* to point out
the background gawpers that would be in shot.

At the station a film crew watch a replay
of a girl in a close-up tantrum and as she
strides across to join them I tell her she
looks like Lollobrigida but she says she's
never heard of her so I tidy a cable under
a mat to stop people tripping over.

And strolling home along Bankside
watch dusk flooded away by arc lights
as a crinolined lady teases the hero
but after the fifth take I leave
thinking you'd still be with me
if you knew I was big in movies.

Random Spanish Lesson

Half way up the stairs to the launch, the toilet,
stench, turbo jet drier, speaker in the ceiling:
say English *Ingles* do you understand?
entiendes? you do not understand
no intiendo do you speak Spanish?
habla Español?

In the room, a malice of poets, swirl of pearls
and jeans, a weariness of *shards* and *souls*,
adjectival gluts, neo-surrealism dwelling in its
own arse, and the high voice, rising terminals,
'We see Rokohiv after Samothrace,
Free of Pisistratus,
Oh! bright Apollo...'

Down the stairs again,
the half open door,
no inttiendo
no intiendo

Rewind

War Poet

That war stuff.
He knew all the phrases,
like, '*cold earth hiding
corpses like winter seeds.*'
and, '*still eyes blanking Heaven*'
also (one he particularly liked)
'*The tease and doubt of shelling*'

Sat huddled round a brown
fireplace he fingered books
with glee and sipped tea
often from a khaki bottle
while she shuffle-slippered
admiringly around him
dusting flags in the map on the wall.

For some reason unbeknown
they sent for him. Had to go,
though didn't have a good war.
In the end apparently screamed
(from a shell-shattered face)
'*What the fucking blazes..?*
Yep, he knew all the phrases.

Breakdown

In sweatpanic terror you plead
for entrance at the local Bedlam
where you see a man die
on your first night
and they take your dental floss away.

Led onto wet grass in the morning
a white coat pedals up
and asks if you bite your nails.
We'll soon make you better he says,
cycle clips tight and tidy.

But you stay months,
needle-pierced in early dawns
drifting into insulin-deep sleeps
because they don't drop you
into cold baths any more
and playing football by order
with a sugar water bottle in your fist
to defy instant comas,
watching a crazed goalkeeper
stopping shots with his face.

You dig the hospital allotment
without knowing why
and someone from Ward 4
scrapes a pick across a long-stay's scalp,
blood covering his smiling teeth.

The stiff dances in F Ward
with glazed eyed girls
are no incentive to leave
your glass-walled mind,
and your silent screams are just as loud.

Baggage

Lying next to you
as your hands express themselves
against dawn curtains
(a change from your five a.m. hooverings)
knowing that this moment
will be stuck with others
like labels on luggage.

Sitting legsplayed on a stool
restless fingers drumming
you dance over my egos
and whirl through walls
until we both weary
and mumble about where we're going.

I wanna travel light.
Want you off my case.

Teachertalk

Victorian town hall, Colonial masturbation;
Ionic capitals, swags, tongue and dart,
pedagogic Inspector lady with too much make-up
putting aitches in front of aitches
while I cynically await the buzz words of Edu-biz.

But, smiling simplicity,
no *provision of disparate subject modules,*
or *quantifiable non-arbitrary criteria of
resource-based parameters* and why no
pro-active focusing, and why did you
slam out of the house this morning
screaming that you were never real to me
and that I intellectualize everything when

of course I don't. And now we're off to
Beefeaterharvesterland where tatoo shouldered
Essex mangirls cackle into mobiles
and skins with beemers chardonnay on about
the A12, mini heart and dolphin earrings jingling
as they strut, sitting down, at the bar
and an old man with a Los Angeles Raiders
baseball cap bores on about his caravan, and
your deep eyes imploring me to join in and
stop *observing* and why don't I see *you* and

I wonder if you'll still be there
when I get home.

Edge

I hate wearing ties.
Given the choice
between a Masonic do
and an anti-capitalist demo
I'd go for the trashings.

I hate capitalists.
I fucked one once.
Bitch.
(I really wanted to shag
an Art Deco cinema
but I was too pissed)
It was in the tabloids.
I saved the cuttings.

I'm a political slut.
I love anarchists
and I love the Masons.
They've got great handshakes
and I love the way their women
dress up for functions.

I had an affair with
a Worshipful Master,
told him I was
a leather-clad activist.
I used to pin badges on his penis
that said *Up The Revolution*.
He loved it.
Like I said
I'm a slut.

Greenfingers

The fern you brought me
before you left
is now cascading
over the table.
I watch it. Withering.

The yucca in the corner
turns away embarrassed
hiding its leaves
against the wall
pretending not to notice.

The mantelshelf ivy
creeps towards
the TV seeking
escapist entertainment
and trying not to say
I told you so.

Swaying slowly
the spider plant
waits to devour me.
But like you it
probably won't bother.

Rhetoric

There are words I don't wish you to use
he announces, exploding the silence.
natural progress bad good
right wrong shouldn't should
Why? Someone. Come on.
His authority fills the hall.

They're value judgements, that's why
and we don't know what they mean,
we haven't a hotline to God.
(he sneeringly emphasises 'God').
This is Social Science. We create
the illusion that we can distance
ourselves from the world and make
objective comments upon it by a style
of expression in which 'I' is not used.
His audience smiles uneasily, wondering
if they have enough words *left* to use.

He'd noticed the girl at the front
as soon as he'd strutted to the lectern
but had turned his head towards everyone
except her, until now, when her eyes
snare his and she quietly asks
What about 'I' as in, say, 'I love you?'

He hesitates, then continues. We call
that an *affectual tie* or the Freudian
an overestimation of the sex object
but they are not quantifiable and we are
not interested in qualitative experience.

His voice has quickened, is louder, harsher
as if, somehow, he is trying to survive.

Different Now

I'll have no truck said the trucker
with truckabilia.
No pagethrees and fifties pics
of scantyclad Swedish beauties
(the only Nord Babe I want
is this Scania FLZ 18 DIESEL.
eightygrandsworth of ABS,
synchromesh, kitchen sink, the lot).

The old 'uns 'll tell yer about it;
the birds, that 'ride for a ride' stuff,
the caffs, heartattacksonaplate.
Family man meself. Snaps of me kids
in me cab and 'er indoors on the door.
I'm professional. HGV'd. I don't get
up cars' arses. Intimidate. Mate.

Anyway, hop in luv. Hope those tight
jeans are clean, don't dirty me seat.
Right, here we go. Smooth innit?
D'you like it smooth? Hardly know
we're movin'. I move well. Know what
I mean? You got buttons or a zip…
Oh, come *on*! You stood there with -

Keep *still*. I'm pullin' over.
Wanna do yer.
Gonna screw yer.
Lay yer.
Play yer.
Slay yer.

Walkover

My daughters
with their clearformed faces
that glowing fullness of cheek
longloose hair tossing.
Laughing. With him.

He's foreign. Oh yes.
Called one day and offered to tame our garden.
Lives opposite. Has a pit bull.
Shouts at it, shapes it, becomes it.
It has resentful eyes. His are large,
mock sad, slyly innocent.
He shrugs wide shoulders,
curls lips in a dark stubbled face.

He takes them to the park each day with the dog.
I have tales to tell you he says.
Do you love me Hannah? he asks of my youngest.
And you Lorna. You smile now
he grins with female coyness.
And it is so. Both are transformed.
The little one skips and whistles,
the eldest blooms. Sparkeyed, smilewide lips.

And I come home to his thicklegged sprawl
his arms fleshed around their young shoulders
their eyes on that absurdly curling hair
as I pass to kiss their mother's mouth
knowing one day it too will smile
and she will walk with him and my daughters.
And their green eyes will be foreign to me.

Doubt

Never been *really* sure.
Had some clues though:
a male model glimpsed in an art class
long legged Eurasian youths
curly haired teenaged twins
their tight jeans prettyboying them along
their provocative pavement
and, once, the flash of a scaffolder's buttock.

But then, there was the girl I watched
walk gloriously out of Women's Studies
tossing an auburn mane in derision.
And the women who don't quite
cross their legs on underground trains.
Even the sepia thrill of a Victorian nude.

I've heard that when two people are
attracted to each other at a party
the man may rhythmically skim a finger
round the rim of his wine glass
whilst the female gently massages
the stem of hers between fingers and thumb.

And here at the end-of-term do
I sip my drink and am entranced
by the lilting profiles
of the Principal's daughter
and the slim man from Admin
leaning against the wall.

Oops!

Butterfingers.

Metaphysics

My lover and I.
She has amber hair, honeycoloured skin
my hair is dark - tinged perfectly with grey
we have lovely smiles
(she has two more teeth than me but mine are whiter).
We are slim and healthy, tall and beautiful.
We make things.

She crafts ceramic brooches from curds and whey
filigree earrings from chocolate mousse.
fine bracelets from lilac leaves
is well known for the intricate rings
she makes from moon dust.

I paint murals full of cricketers playing on clouds
ceilings of sky hanging with chandeliers of fire.
I fashion lyrics from starlings feathers and sunrays
and wave my hand for sonnets to appear.

We wanted to work together, in concert,
made him with such gentleness and passion
willed him in such glorious imaginings
that he was born in the arms of angels,
and they danced on the heads of pins.

Rewind

At dawn I draw the curtains and roll into bed
where I dream till the previous evening
of old trains sucking smoke from the sky
and stopping when the man
lowers his green flag.

During the day my shaver
plants bristles in my chin
and my teeth produce foam
which I remove perfectly with a brush
after backcombing my hair into disarray.

Looking at where I've come from
I ease into a classroom
where students ask answers
before I give questions
and make notes before I speak.

And I feel the pain before I see you
silently pass along the corridor
and remember that soon
I will bump out of you again.

What

What happened to you?
To what you are from where you were.
I hardly noticed. The change was slow.
Silent. No ripple. Hardly a stir.

Where are the kids? Isn't one in China?
They got tall, didn't they. Grew so fast.
We didn't see Timmy much.
But they did leave home. Us. At last.

Though we got by, didn't we?
Life, like the economy, slump and boom.
Where are you then? Is something wrong?
I'm standing here in an empty room.

TITLES

Lightning Source UK Ltd.
Milton Keynes UK
UKOW02f1919221015

261195UK00001BA/140/P